FINANCIAL 180

GIVE GENEROUSLY,
SAVE CONSISTENTLY,
LIVE WISELY

JASON CLINE

Financial 180: Give Generously, Save Consistently, Live Wisely

Jason Cline
103 Bledsoe Drive
Hendersonville, TN 37075

ISBN - 979-8-9852476-0-2 (paperback)
979-8-9852476-1-9 (ebook)

Editing and design by ChristianEditingAndDesign.com.

Table of Contents

Acknowledgments

First and foremost, I'd like to thank my Heavenly Father for all You've done for me. You sent Your Son to die for me, and You continue to love me even though I don't deserve it. You've blessed me in so many ways. Help me to always follow Your two greatest commandments—love You and love others.

I'd also like to thank my family—especially my wife, Jamie; and my kids, Kinley and Ty. You know me better than anyone else, and you still love me. I'm so proud of what you've done, and I look forward to seeing what God has in store for you in the future.

Finally, I'd like to thank my friends who encouraged me to write this book. I want to especially thank Brian Harrell, Bubba Hooker, and Jason Gibson. You were a huge help when I was creating this process, and you kept telling me to write this book. I didn't have the confidence needed to do this, but you kept pushing me. Thank you so much.

Introduction

I was born in the small town of Westmoreland, Tennessee, in 1975. Westmoreland was a lot like Mayberry from *The Andy Griffith Show* (my favorite show growing up). It was a unique little town where everyone knew you and your family. People would watch out for you and your family too.

Westmoreland was a simple place to live. I remember our town getting a Hardee's when I was in high school, and that was a big deal. Now that I'm older, I sometimes long for those simpler times, and I have to admit: I had a great life growing up. We didn't have much, but we had what we needed. I had three best friends all throughout my childhood: Nathan, Griff, and Adam. It's cool that we still keep in contact today.

I always loved sports growing up. I played football, basketball, and baseball. As I got older, football became my number-one sport. I was very active in clubs and school organizations as well, which was easy because I lived so close to my school from seventh through twelfth grade. I had a two-minute walk to school each day. The football field was beside my house, and I remember smelling my dad's pork chops on the grill while I was at practice. Both my parents were always at my football games. I can remember my mom coming to a game just a couple of days after a major surgery. I couldn't believe she was there, but it was so important to her.

My parents always took us to church, and I'm so thankful for that. At the age of fifteen I preached my first sermon at church. I knew that ministry would always be a part of my life.

After graduating from high school, I attended Tennessee Tech University in Cookeville, Tennessee. My time in college was one of the best experiences of my life. I'd never been away from home for a long period of time, so the beginning was a huge adjustment. Cookeville was so much bigger than Westmoreland. I remember calling Pizza Hut my first week to order a pizza and they asked if I wanted it delivered. I thought they were joking because when I was growing up we had to drive thirty minutes to get a pizza.

After a couple of weeks I found a group of friends and became heavily involved with the Fellowship of Christian Athletes (FCA). I'd been involved in FCA in middle school and high school, but my time in college was an unforgettable experience. The relationships I formed in FCA at Tech helped me grow so much as a man. I learned a lot about myself during this time.

I majored in education because I wanted to be a math teacher and football coach. I also got to work with the football team. For the first couple of years I was a manager, but later I had the opportunity to work as a student coach.

After college I moved to Hendersonville, Tennessee, which was about forty-five minutes away from my hometown. I was fortunate enough to get a job at Hendersonville High School in 1998. This is where I started my career as a high school math teacher and football coach. I was young, living in an apartment with a good friend named Jason (yes, we had the same name). At the same time, Jason did a great job managing his money, and I used to make fun of him for it. I'd say, "Dude, you're way too extreme with that budgeting. I bet you write down the cost of a pack of gum." Jason wrote down everything he spent, and I couldn't understand why. All I knew was that wasn't for me. He was already saving for retirement at the age of twenty-three. He didn't have any debt, and he was so disciplined with his money. I thought he wasn't having enough fun.

You see, although I felt pretty good about myself and was doing adult things, I had no clue what I was doing when it came to my finances. So I was quite the opposite of Jason. I just spent freely what money I made. I traded trucks at least once a year, and my payment kept growing higher and higher (I wasted so much money on vehicle payments). Either I had a student loan that was in default, or I was just paying the minimum monthly payment. I did use cash, but not the right way. I'd go to the ATM and get out $40–$60 and go back whenever that was gone (sometimes that afternoon or maybe the next day). I never kept track of where the money was going. I wasn't saving any money, and I wasn't giving anything to my church or a charity. I was single, and with my extra time I worked a few extra jobs, but the money I earned was wasted too. This cycle continued until 2003.

As I look back at those days living with Jason, I have to be honest. I'd never learned how to budget money. My parents never taught me, and I didn't seem to pick it up anywhere while living in Westmoreland or in college. The other part of the story is this: I don't think my parents ever learned—or were ever taught—how to manage money either. I eventually learned, but I did so the hard way.

2003: A New Beginning

2003 was a big year for me. I got married in March to my wife, Jamie. I was still teaching math and coaching football, and Jamie was a teacher as well. We bought a house, of course, but I still had no clue how to manage money. We were both also working on our master's degrees, which wasn't cheap. So now we had a mortgage, student loans, credit card debt, and a truck payment. I was thankful that Jamie entered our marriage with no debt, but she really didn't have a desire to handle our finances. All Jamie knew was not to spend more than she made, but that still left me in charge of the finances. I'll put it plainly: it wasn't working. We were drowning, and I knew that something had to change. Financially, I had to do a "180." I had to totally change the way I was handling our money and go the other direction.

This didn't happen overnight, but little by little we started to see change. If I remember correctly, we had about $40,000 of debt (truck, student loan, and credit cards), not including the house. I started working extra jobs, and we paid off the $40K in about eighteen months. We finished our master's degrees without taking on more debt. Now we were debt free except for the house, and I knew I didn't want to go back into debt. After all our hard work, we could now give money to our church and put money into savings. Sure, there were new challenges we'd have to face. We'd have to learn how to communicate as a couple about money and avoid trying to keep up with the Joneses. We'd also become parents in 2007 and again in 2008, which we learned was way more expensive than we ever thought.

Since both of us worked full time, our kids would go to daycare. I had no clue how expensive this would be. Then there were diapers, formula, doctors' visits, and so much more. It seemed like we were at the doctor's office at least one or two times a week. Owning a house was more expensive than I thought too. We always had maintenance to do and things to buy for the house. When Jamie and I first got married, I could write our grocery list on a Post-it Note. Now I was having to using a sheet of notebook paper.

Flash Forward: 2021

Fast forward eighteen years later. We have two kids—ages fourteen and twelve. I work for a nonprofit, and Jamie is an elementary school librarian. I feel like most of our life is pretty simple. We live about a mile away from most of the things we need. Our church is across the street (I walk most of the time). Our kids' school is a mile down the road, and so are the grocery store, the gas station, and several restaurants. There are still some crazy parts from time to time, but I try to keep things as simple as possible.

We have no debt except for a small mortgage. We have our emergency fund saved. We contribute the max amount each month into our Individual Retirement Accounts (IRAs) and our Health Savings Account (HSA). We now own older vehicles—which is hilarious to me. Having a newer truck was always so important to me. I'd get tired of the one I was driving and want something new. I didn't care what the payment was. It was just a part of life. Now my truck is twelve years old and Jamie's car is ten years old, and I'm okay with that. Those things aren't important to me anymore. So despite the irony, we're saving money each month to buy Jamie a new car when our daughter turns sixteen. The plan is to give our daughter Jamie's old vehicle rather than purchase another new car. My goodness—I've become a lot more practical as I've gotten older.

I now divide our paychecks into three parts: Give, Save, and Live. Most of our paychecks go toward giving and saving. We're currently giving and saving around 40 percent of our take-home pay. Each month we can save for vacation, Christmas, holidays, birthdays, retirement, and a newer car for Jamie. We can give money to our church and support a few of our friends who work for a nonprofit and have to raise their own financial support. We have money in our budget that we call "other giving" that allows us to help people or ministries as needs arise. We live on a lot less than what we make, and that, my friends, is the key not just to turning it all around but to maintaining a healthy financial lifestyle. Therefore, this is one of the things I'll touch on throughout this book.

Finally, the main things I wish to show you in this book are the Four Stages of Finances, which correspond to the Give, Save, and Live I mentioned above. The Four Stages of Finances are Drowning, Treading, Swimming, and Wading. Throughout the book, there are tips, tricks, and questions you can ask yourself so you can figure out where you are in these stages. In turn, you'll learn how to get to the next step.

I've lived through this myself, so I know what it's like. So many people are drowning in their finances. I remember clearly what it's like when you can't breathe and don't know where to turn. It's my hope that this book will allow you to do what I did eighteen years ago—turn it all around and take a financial 180. I've never looked back, and I pray that you can do the same!

—Jason Cline
August 21, 2021

1

Simplify

"Get all the advice and instructions you can, so you will be wise the rest of your life."[1]

As you can probably tell by now, my favorite word is *simplify*. I don't like for things to be complicated. Unfortunately, I've made some decisions in my life that didn't help things to be simple. Every day we make a lot of decisions. Some are big and some are small. Some decisions we don't really have to think about—you know: the kinds of decisions that aren't really going to impact your day. For example, where I go eat lunch isn't a complicated decision. However, there are some decisions that can cause our lives to be more complicated—but also simpler, for that matter.

Looking back, I think about some of the decisions I've made over the years related to my professional career. Sometimes it's easy to believe that the grass is greener on the other side, but I've learned it's usually not. I'd take a job only to regret it a few months later. Over the last twenty-plus years, I've had a few different jobs. I've worked in education, at my church, and for two different nonprofit ministries. I've changed jobs because I was bored or frustrated or because I wanted more money. Here are two things I've learned: no job is perfect, and making more money doesn't guarantee more happiness.

Another thing I've learned is that I need to take my time when making big decisions. I can be excited about anything for a few days. The real test for me is seeing if I'm still excited in a week or two. If I am, there may be something to this decision. Most of the time, though, I've already forgotten about what was exciting me just a few days before. If I'd made a quick decision, I probably would've done something I'd end up regretting. I've done that many times in my life.

I've used this same process when hiring staff over the years. When I was on staff with FCA, someone would ask me about working there almost every week. After explaining the job description, I'd tell them to pray and think about it for about two weeks. I asked them to call me back if they still felt strongly about pursuing a job at FCA after that time. The ones who contacted me after two weeks all came on staff. I'd say this number was about 2 percent. I never heard from the others, and that's okay. All of them found the job they were supposed to take for that particular time in their lives.

I feel that this is a great example about how we need to be careful when making big decisions. Take your time. In fact, take a couple of weeks. Then, if you're still excited, proceed. This is especially true for dealing with your finances and making major purchases.

I've met with many individuals and couples over the years to help them with their finances. I hate to say it, but most of them have made decisions that really complicated their finances. Most of the time they have a huge car payment (usually around $500 a month). This can really complicate your life. For example, if you're paying $500 a month on something that's going down in value, chances are, you owe more on the car than it was worth. These are the kinds of things that can be avoided if you take the time to make decisions about things. Trust me: this will simplify your life.

I believe that life was made to be simple. A few bad decisions can put you in a very tough spot. No doubt about it: one bad decision, and you're stuck paying for it for months (if not years). So here's the good news: simplicity is the key to finding financial freedom. If you made mistakes with your finances, that's okay. We can change that. Sure, you can't change the past, but you can turn things around and change what's going to happen in the future. I'm here for you, and I promise to help keep this process of getting your life back on the road a simple one. Finally, I'll help you get to where you want to be.

2

Give, Save, Live

"Look straight ahead, and fix your eyes on what lies before you. Mark out a straight path for your feet; stay on the safe path."[2]

A few years ago my son had a piggy bank made up of three different pieces. Each piece had a word on it. One said "Give," another said "Save," and the other said "Spend." I couldn't help but notice that this was an ideal way to organize my own budget. For a kid, it really is that simple; but for adults, budgets are that much more complicated because we have so much more to think about. Like I said in the previous chapter, however, we must simplify. Therefore, to live a more well-rounded life, I believe we should do three things when we get paid: Give, Save, and Live.

We should give some of our money to help others who are less fortunate than we are. We should save money in an emergency fund for those unexpected expenses that come up at the most inconvenient times. Finally, we should live on the rest. Unfortunately, the living part can get way out of hand. I've tried to teach this to my kids. I've also coached many adults on this living part, and the truth of the matter is, most humans are really good at the living part but not so good at the saving and the giving.

Before we go in depth in the three areas, I'd like to begin by saying that I think everyone will be fine with the Save and the Live. Sometimes the Give is a little harder to understand. You might ask, "Why should I give?" Here's a short story to answer that very question.

Back in 2006, *60 Minutes* did an interview with NFL quarterback Tom Brady. Tom was twenty-seven years old and had already won three Super Bowls. He was on top of the world. I'm sure he had plenty of money in the bank and could buy anything he wanted. I'll never forget what Tom said: "Why do I have three Super Bowl rings and still think there's something greater out there for me?" He went on to say, "It's got to be more than this." When asked what the answer was, Tom said, "I wish I knew."[3]

Tom is right; there's got to be more to life. I'm here to fill in that answer: I believe the answer is giving. When we die, we can't take anything with us, after all. We can save as much money as possible and buy the biggest houses and toys, but we'll leave it all behind. The best thing we can do during our lives is to help others by giving our money and our time.

I recently looked at my first budget from when Jamie and I had just gotten married. It had a little bit of giving, not much saving, and a whole lot of living. I can see now that my life would look totally different today if I hadn't done a financial 180 and changed my ways many years ago. Jamie and I give to our church and other ministries we're passionate about. So the giving has become a vital part of our lives, and we enjoy doing it. For example, lately we've increased our giving and done so by giving more cash. Just the other night my family went on an overnight retreat to Nashville. Jamie and I both had cash on us, and we could give generous tips to our server and a musician at the Opryland Hotel. It's nice to be able to give a good tip to someone who does a great job. It's even nicer to do it and not have to worry about not being able to pay another bill because of it.

Saving has changed for us in the last few years. Our savings used to be all about an emergency fund. At first we had no emergency fund to pay for those unexpected expenses. Then we'd have a small emergency fund saved and something would break or quit working. We consistently saw our emergency fund go from $1,000 back to zero. Finally we could start saving consistently, and now we have our six-month emergency fund in place. Now we can save for other things that are important to us, like vacations, holidays, and vehicles.

The living is everything else: housing, insurance, groceries, gas, vehicles, entertainment, and so on. The living part has been the biggest adjustment for me. I had so many bad habits I had to change. When I got out of college, I'd buy something without really worrying about the price. I would just put it on credit and pay the minimum payments. I've already mentioned that I didn't make good decisions about vehicles. I was also the same way with my cell phone, eating out, activities with friends, etc. I'd charge these things to my credit card and pay it off a little at a time. I'd end up paying so much more because of interest. So many things don't mean as much to me as they used to. I no longer have to buy the latest cell phone or have the highest cable TV package. I've learned to live on older items that are just as good.

I started organizing my budget this way and have taught others to do the same. A good, simple goal to start with is to Give 10 percent, Save 10 percent, and Live on 80 percent of your income. Many can't start there, but that's okay. I always tell people to start where you can and work toward this over time. As you decrease the living, increase the giving and saving. Like I mentioned in the first chapter, sometimes you have to really think hard about major decisions. This is one of those, but I promise: if you commit to this simple method, it'll be a decision you'll never regret.

3

Paydays and Due Dates

"Pride leads to conflict;
those who take advice are wise."[4]

Over the next four chapters we'll discuss the Four Stages of Finances: Drowning, Treading, Swimming, and Wading. But before we figure out which stage you're in, let's talk about something that can get really confusing for most who've been living paycheck to paycheck. An overwhelming sense of confusion can happen when you start to get everything organized. When you start to budget, one of the first things that needs to be done is to add up the number of paychecks your family has coming in each month. Then you must get your timing right. Let's look at a strategy I've come up with to make this a simpler task.

The First Half & Second Half Strategy

Some people get paid once per month. This makes the budgeting process a lot easier, but the downside is that it's sometimes hard to make the money last a whole month (especially when you first start budgeting). On the other hand, some people get paid every week. Sure, it's nice to have money coming in every week, but this can also be tricky. Let's look at some examples.

My wife and I both get paid once per month, but mine is at the end of the month. Her paycheck comes through on the 15th. It took some work to figure this out, but what we do is divide our budget by two. We have a first-half-month budget and a second-half-month budget. Then we figure out the due dates of all our bills and expenses and put each in the right budget. Some things like gas and groceries are actually in both parts of the budget.

Another example is when couples get paid twice a month on the same days. You can handle this the same way Jamie and I do. You just have a first-half budget and a second-half budget. However, it gets really complicated when a couple has different paydays.

The "Leave It Alone" Strategy

I've seen couples in which one person gets paid on the 1st and 15th and the other one gets paid every other Friday. You might be thinking, "Does that mean I have to do four budgets?" If you recall, I'm all about making things simple, so the answer is no—that would be way too complicated. In this case, I also suggest a couple make a first-half budget and a second-half budget. But what if the first person gets paid on the 1st and the other gets paid on the 5th this month? Would you then make another budget for those five days?

I always say I love budgeting but don't want to do it all the time—again, too complicated. Therefore, the answer to the question above is no. Again, we're trying to simplify. The answer to the above scenario is to leave that money alone. The simplest thing is to wait and do your budget on the 5th. The easiest thing to do is for the one who gets paid on the 1st of the month to leave their deposit alone and not do anything for four days. Then, in the second half of the month, if one person gets paid on the 15th and the other gets paid on the 19th, they would wait until the 19th to start that new budget.

The Week-to-Week Example

Again, I love budgeting, but you don't want to have four budgets. It's too much of a headache. So the same rules apply for the toughest example I have seen so far. That's when both people get paid weekly. When you get paid weekly, it's convenient for things like gas, groceries, and spending money. You do those things every week. It gets more complicated with your bills like the mortgage, utilities, debts, and insurance. If you take the first check each month and pay your house payment, you may not have any money left for gas or groceries. You don't want to do that to yourself. Here's an example of how to handle this scenario.

You can open additional bank accounts and use them for budgeting purposes. For example, I had one couple open an account at the bank for their monthly expenses. We then divided up all their expenses by four. Consequently, if their mortgage and utilities totaled $1,600 per month, they would move $400 per week into the new account. Then when the bill was due, they would pay it out of that account. This turned a complicated issue into an easy plan.

Your Own Reality

People's situations are different. You may be in a scenario where you don't know when you're going to get paid. In that case, you may need to alter these strategies. Sure, some people like getting paid once per month and others like getting paid weekly, but your preferences are usually a result of what you're used to. Whatever the case, the important thing is to keep your budget simple. The more complicated it is, the less chance you'll stick with it.

4

Drowning

"Plans go wrong for lack of advice;
many advisers bring success."[5]

I've always had a fear of drowning. It seems to me that all humans have the fear ingrained in their DNA—the old sink-or-swim scenario. I remember being in the ocean when I was a kid and having a wave take me off my feet. Even though I wasn't in very deep water, the undertow was too strong for me. The power of the tide pulled me underwater! I remember vividly how I had to fight to get back to the surface. Sometimes I got lucky and would just stand up and I'd be okay, but then there were those scary times I'd realize I was in too deep and couldn't touch the bottom. If just for a moment, I was out of control; I was drowning.

Here's another memory: when I was a very young child, my parents used to take us to Cave City, Kentucky. Three or four families from our church would go together and spend the weekend. We'd stay at the Cave Land Motel and swim a lot in the pool. I remember one weekend while we were there, everyone else was swimming and having a good time, but I wasn't since I couldn't swim. I had that floatable ring around my waist keeping me above the water. I can't remember how, but something happened and I turned upside down. I felt like I was drowning. Suddenly my Aunt Wanda turned me right-side up and I was okay. That's one of those stories I'll never forget.

My parents worked very hard so that they could take us on these weekend trips. Neither had a lot of education, but they wanted to provide for us. They did the best they could do with what they had. Dad joined the army after high school and then went to college for one quarter (this was before semesters). When Dad got back home, he and Mom got married, but she was still in high school. She quit school at age sixteen and started working. Mom did go back and get her GED, when I was in middle school, I believe. I was so proud of her for doing that because it gave her more opportunities in her professional life.

Hard Times Come

I remember when Dad lost his job at the Tennessee Valley Authority. I was young and didn't know the details, but I can remember Dad telling me he'd changed roles, which caused him to lose his seniority. Soon after, there was a layoff, and he lost his job.

The next thing I remember was Dad taking a job for the city of Westmoreland. Evidently he took a big cut in pay, and my parents weren't prepared for it. I believe that was the year my parents had to borrow money from a friend to buy us Christmas presents. That had to be hard for them. I know this was one of many sacrifices they made so that my brother and I could have the things we needed and wanted. Looking back, I see now that my parents were drowning in their finances, and I'm pretty sure they didn't know what to do.

This is true for many people: they're drowning when it comes to their finances. They're underwater and can't breathe. They need someone to come alongside them and turn them back over—much like my aunt did for me—but in this case, you're going to have to do it for yourself. Therefore, the first thing you have to do is to get your head above water. To do so, you must first learn what it looks like to be drowning financially. The second step is to figure out where you are—how far underwater you actually are. Then we can look at the next step that'll get you in a better place.

> **GIVE:**
> **When you're drowning, you can't give consistently.**

This may seem too obvious to some, but not to others: if you're drowning, you can't give consistently. On the other hand, giving financially may not be important to you, but as I stated earlier, it's a good idea. As you read through this book, I hope you'll recognize that giving back financially can be a top priority for you and your family.

The question is, why do we need to give? For one, giving allows us to make a difference in the lives of others. There's always someone else who's in worse shape than you. I've always been told that if you live in the United States, you're richer than most other people in the world. Sometimes it's hard to see this when we're struggling, but it's true. Even if it's just a little amount, giving can make a huge difference in the life of someone else.

Giving has always been very important to me. Every job I've ever had was about helping people. I enjoy working with someone and helping them get from where they are to where they want to be. It's frustrating to me when people just give up when they're so close to achieving success. I feel like I've always been a giver; I just wasn't always a giver financially. I was very good at spending money on myself for things that really didn't matter or things that I'd get tired of pretty quickly. I liked when people did something nice for me, like buying my dinner or giving me a gift, but I was never good at returning the favor. I didn't realize at the time what a blessing it was to be able to do something nice for someone without expecting anything in return. When someone needed me to help them by giving my time, I was fine with that. I just didn't want to give any money to help out another person or organization. I didn't really see the value. I'm so thankful I'm not that way anymore.

I can remember meeting with a couple who were drowning financially a couple of years ago. The thing that broke the woman's heart more than anything else was not being able to give. I could tell that this was a top priority for her. This gave her motivation to start moving forward. It was also a lesson for me to learn. At first I wanted to tell her that she just couldn't give in this stage of her life. That would've deflated her, and I probably wouldn't have met with this couple again to help them move forward with their finances.

I've been so blessed in my life. When Jamie and I got married in 2003, we were both teaching school. It was very important for us to try to give 10 percent of our income to our church, but because I'd gotten myself into such bad shape financially, it was a stretch each month. Some months it didn't happen. My point in telling you all this is simple: we were drowning, and therefore, we *couldn't give* every time we wanted to. Thus, if you find yourself in this kind of scenario, then you're drowning.

> **SAVE:**
> **When you're drowning, you have little or no money saved for an emergency.**

When you're drowning financially, you can't save money consistently. If you have a savings account, there may be little or nothing in it. This is a tough spot to be in, and I've been there. For a lot of folks, saving may not be a priority. They've been living paycheck to paycheck for so long that they don't even think about it. So the question is this: why should we want to save money?

I can answer this question with one word: *emergencies!* Every week something breaks in my house. If you have kids, you can totally relate. Many things can be called emergencies: your car breaks down; you have an unexpected medical expense; an appliance in your house decides to quit working. The list keeps going on and on, and I promise it won't stop growing. Let me give you an example.

I remember a time when I was so excited that we'd saved a few thousand dollars in our emergency fund. I'd never done this before. I was feeling so confident, but then life happened. In one week our emergency fund went from several thousand dollars to just a few hundred dollars. In one sense I was so thankful that we had the money to pay for it, but I was still devasted because now I had to start all over.

LIVE:
When you're drowning, you're living paycheck to paycheck, you don't have a budget, and you possibly can't pay the minimum payments on your debt.

Knowing what this is like, whenever I meet with people to help them with their finances, I always ask how much they have in their savings for emergencies. Most of the time they don't have anything in their savings for emergencies—or anything at all in savings, for that matter. Also, most of the time they've come to me for guidance regarding their finances because of an emergency that's happened in their lives. A lot of times they've had multiple emergencies. This is the main reason to save, I tell them.

Another reason to save is for things you want to do in the future: take vacations, buy Christmas presents, and so on. Without savings you can't move on to the next step, which is the living stage. Think about it this way: if you're drowning, you're not really living. Therefore, you must *save* yourself from drowning by *saving*.

When you're drowning financially, what does your *living* look like? You're probably living paycheck to paycheck, which is a hard place to be. It seems there's never enough money to buy the things you need. It seems there's always too much left to pay at the end of the month. Not only are you living paycheck to paycheck, but you probably can't pay the minimum payments on your debt. The balance just keeps growing every month because you can't pay the interest on the loan. Each month you're just sinking deeper and deeper.

I remember getting out of college and having a student loan of several thousand dollars. At first I started paying the minimum balance, but eventually I just let it go on default. I didn't know that the interest was still growing and I was going to have to pay back more. I see folks doing this all the time and hate to see them in this kind of shape.

Another thing I see that causes people to drown is the vehicles they drive. Like I mentioned in the introduction, so many people have at least a $500 car payment. That eats up a lot of their budget. As you know, this was a big weakness of mine when I got out of college. I never bought a new truck (thankfully), but I'd trade vehicles all the time. I'd drive a truck for a few months and get tired of it. Then I'd go down to the car dealership and buy another one. I can remember trading trucks twice in one week one time. For many years, I owed more on the truck than it was worth. I believe my highest payment was $450 a month. Looking back on that now, it was crazy!

I have another friend who's always had an issue with trading trucks. One problem is that he always buys a brand-new truck. Another problem is that he gets one of the title loans to buy something else. When he doesn't pay the payment, they come after his truck. Recently he bought a brand-new $50,000 truck and has a payment that's at least $600 a month for the next seven years. That's pretty crazy too.

Here's an example crazier than that: I met with a couple who had two car payments totaling $1,600 a month. The worse news was that they owed around $60,000 on two cars that were worth no more than $20,000 together. These two expenses were more than their house payment! That isn't living, friends!

Why do we let ourselves get into such situations? In our modern world we've learned that we don't have to wait. We're all about instant gratification. It's like this: we can finance items now for eight to ten years, so why wait and save up? If you're drowning, the last thing you need to think about is buying something you don't really need or don't have the money to pay for. That's how people start drowning in the first place. Like I mentioned earlier, take some time and think about this decision. In a few days you'll probably forget all about it.

I'm so thankful I quit trading trucks. The last two trucks I've bought have been paid for with cash. It's a great feeling when you're leaving the car lot and you don't owe them anything. My truck now is twelve years old and has over 200,000 miles. The great thing is that I'm fine with that. I recently had the opportunity to buy a friend's truck. It was only two years old and had only 30,000 miles on it. Years ago I would've gone to the bank and taken out a loan to buy it. Instead, I thought about it for a few days and decided it wasn't the best decision. The moral of the story is this: buying vehicles is a luxury that can cause you to keep drowning if you're not careful.

The "B" Word

Another common factor in why we're drowning is that we don't have a plan. Yes, I'm talking about the "B" word: *budget.* If you've never used a budget, it can be a tough thing to start. I don't believe you can manage your finances without some sort of plan.

Today there are so many options for budgeting. You can use a budgeting app, or you can print out a budget. For me, I'm still a fan of the Excel spreadsheet. Even though I'm a math guy and love numbers, I use Excel because it does the math for me and it's so easy to make an adjustment. I still have my very first budget, and I look at it from time to time. It makes me laugh to see how little I knew about spreadsheets and budgets twenty years ago. The key thing was that I just kept going. The more I did it, the better I got. At any rate, you can use a simple sheet of paper, calculator, and pencil if you wish; it's up to you. But you have to do the budget thing if you want to stop drowning. Remember this: I'm here to help you through; we'll change your life—together.

The Example of Jack and Diane

Throughout this book we're going to use the fictional example of Jack and Diane. They're going to help us walk through what a budget looks like when you're drowning, treading, swimming, and wading. So let's start at the beginning.

Jack and Diane are married and in their forties. They have two kids, one in elementary school and one in middle school. Jack works at a local restaurant, and Diane is an administrative assistant at their son's elementary school. Together they make about $60,000 a year. Jack and Diane both get paid on the last day of the month, which makes the budgeting process so much easier. Jack brings home $2,800, and Diane brings home $1,400, for a total of $4,200 a month.

Financially, they're drowning. They want to take part of their check and use it to help others, but they haven't been able to do that consistently. They have $100 in savings. They have four debts that total $39,000 (not including their house): a vehicle payment, a student loan, a credit card, and a medical bill from a surgery Diane had last year.

Having a lot of debt can take a toll on you and your family. It can cause a lot of stress that can make marriage a lot harder than it already is. Little comments will be made, and over time these little comments can stack up and cause resentment within the relationship.

For Jack and Diane to have the best marriage possible, they have to learn how to communicate about money. They have to be on the same page about getting out of debt. In many situations, one person in the relationship is focused on getting out of debt while the other one isn't on board. This really puts their relationship in a tough spot. Sometimes the one who wants to get out of debt will eventually give up because they can't do it alone. There must be a team approach to achieve success.

One of the first things the team should do, then, is discuss the budget. In Jack and Diane's case, they don't have a budget and have no idea where their money is going each month. Because of that, they're living paycheck to paycheck. Sometimes they have to skip one of their monthly debt payments because they don't have a plan.

So what's the first step to help Jack and Diane? The goal is to get their heads above water; we'll learn more about that in the next chapter. For now, we need to identify all their monthly expenses and the dates they're due. This is their first homework assignment. So when Jack and Diane come back to see me in a week, below is what they've come up with:

1. Mortgage: $1,050
2. Utilities
   - Electric: $150 (average)
   - Water/Sewer: $100 (average)
   - Internet/Cable: $200
   - Cell Phones: $200
3. Truck Payment: $500
4. Student Loan: $125
5. Credit Card: $60
6. Medical Bill: $50

7. Car Insurance: $125
8. Groceries: $1,000 (estimate)
9. Gas: $200 (estimate)
10. Eating Out: $200 (estimate)

Total: $3,960

After seeing all their expenses and learning more about Jack and Diane, I see that they're missing some items and need to make cuts in some areas. To begin, they're not currently giving or saving each month. As I mentioned earlier, they bring home $4,200 a month, and they have no idea where all of that money is going. As you can see above, they know where some of it is going, but some of these were just an estimate (groceries, gas, eating out). I can guarantee they're spending more than $4,200 each month when we get an accurate budget together. In the next chapter we'll take a look at that so that we can help get Jack's and Diane's heads above water.

Challenge: One Step You Can Take Today

Start listing all your monthly expenses and the dates they're due. You probably know an exact amount for several of them, but you'll have to estimate the rest. Just do your best. Over time you'll be able to get a more accurate amount.

5

Treading

"A person without self-control is like a city with broken down walls."[6]

Anytime I've ever been under water, my main goal was to get to the surface. I remember when my dad taught me how to swim. I was probably seven or eight years old, and we were in Cave City, Kentucky. Dad took me out to the hotel pool for my first "swimming lesson." I quickly learned that there was no lesson, just my dad throwing me into the deep end and telling me to swim. I remember struggling at first, but eventually I was able to start treading. My only goal at that time was to keep my head above water. I didn't want to drown. I knew I'd be okay if my head stayed above water.

Getting your head above water is also essential with your finances. It's easy to lose hope if you feel like you're drowning—fear sets in, and things change. We have to decide that we're not going to drown. We have to fight to keep our heads above water. We also need someone close to us who's there to help if we need them. We need someone who's doing well with their finances. We don't need someone who's also drowning to tell us what to do.

When I finally got my head above water, I'd always need a few seconds to compose myself. I'd wipe my eyes and just spend a few seconds catching my breath. Then I could look around and figure out where I was. This provided some stability for me.

The same goes for your finances. When you're drowning financially, you've got to find a way to find some stability. Getting your head above water allows you to catch your breath, compose yourself, and figure out where you are. It also allows you some time to figure out your next steps.

The next step usually involves getting on a plan so that you don't start drowning again. You want to be able to keep your head above water. It's not a plan you can use forever, but it's a whole lot better option than drowning. Therefore, in this chapter we'll talk about what it takes to go from drowning to treading. This is a very important step in your financial life. If you're not careful, you'll go right back underwater and start drowning again. At the same time, if you follow the plan, you won't have to worry about that.

When you were drowning, you couldn't give consistently. One of the steps to move from drowning to treading is to start giving something each month. You might not be able to give much, but you're at least giving consistently. This is a big step. It's important to put this into your budget.

I can remember when I started giving regularly. It wasn't much at all, but it was a consistent amount each month. I was glad to do it, but I have to admit: it was hard to do. Here's why. I was a stingy person. I was more concerned with spending money on things I wanted instead of giving money to others. At that point I just didn't see the value of giving. Sure, I did give my time, but giving money was something that didn't interest me. I didn't see how it benefited me in any way. Boy, was my way of thinking all screwed up!

> **GIVE:**
> **To move from drowning to treading, you have to start giving consistently each month.**

Giving isn't something that comes easily for a lot of people. Especially when you're in debt, you can always justify in your mind that the money should go toward that debt. I do understand that argument, but there's something about giving part of what you earn to help someone else. I know that people have sacrificed for me over the years, and I want to do the same for others.

I've counseled many couples over the years, and most have felt the same way. Their hearts were broken because they couldn't give each month. My encouragement was to give something—to give anything—and do it consistently. I always tell people that as you improve your financial situation, be sure to give a little more.

I mentioned earlier in the book about the 10-10-80 plan, where you divide you finances like this: 10 percent to savings, 10 percent to giving, and 80 percent to living. This plan can be hard at first—especially if you're treading. So don't feel guilty if you can't give 10 percent. I'd rather you give *something* than get frustrated and give nothing at all. If that means you have to start with 1 percent, then start there. As soon as you can, move it up to 2 percent. Eventually, you'll be at the 10 percent or even higher.

Just remember: no one ever started by giving what they give today. They started smaller and grew the amount as they could. Your goal now can be to grow the percentage you give every time you get a chance.

It's essential to have some money in an emergency fund. When an emergency happens (and it will), you'll have some money to pay for it without going more into debt. One thousand dollars will cover most emergencies.

> **SAVE:**
> **To move from drowning to treading, you have to save $1,000 in an emergency fund.**

I remember how I paid for emergencies before I got on the right path. I'd just use my credit card. It was the only way I could pay for it at the time. I'd then pay the minimum amount each month on the card and end up paying a lot more because of interest. I see couples in this situation all the time. Their intention is to pay the card off at the end of the month, but then another emergency happens, and then another. Before they know it, they max out the card and have to move to another. It's hard to move from drowning to treading when you're not saving money each month into your emergency fund.

So it's pretty easy to see what qualifies as an emergency: the tires on your car have to be replaced; one of your kids gets sick and you have to miss work; your refrigerator stops working.

These are all valid emergencies. At the same time you'll be tempted to use your emergency fund for non-emergencies.

What doesn't qualify as an emergency? The biggest one I can think of is eating out too many times. This can break a budget very fast. Paying for expensive hobbies doesn't qualify as an emergency either. I agree that we all need to get away and do fun things, but we can't do these things if they're going to put us in a bad spot with our finances. That's one reason I like to hike. I did buy some good hiking boots, but the actual hiking is free!

Paying for a vacation isn't considered an emergency. Going out of town now is more expensive than ever—just for a weekend. Trust me, friends: I've seen couples over the years who used their emergency fund for a vacation, which caused them to start drowning again.

I also see people who have no emergency fund but have multiple pets at home. I have a miniature Schnauzer named Rosie, and she's my buddy. She's so excited when I get home, and I love her, but she can be very expensive. When people are trying to get their heads above water and they have several animals at home, the process of accumulating savings is much slower. The point is this: I'm not at all saying to give away your pets, but you're going to have to work them into your budget.

So when you get $1,000 saved in this fund, it's important to leave it alone. Like I said, you'll be tempted to use the money for expenses that aren't emergencies, but don't. When something does happen, you'll be thankful you didn't spend it.

LIVE:
To move from drowning to treading, you have to start living on a budget and pay the minimum payments on all your debt.

One of the key steps in moving from drowning to treading is to get on a budget. A budget can be a tough thing to start and can be even tougher to stay on. If you do it, I can promise it'll be one of the greatest decisions you'll ever make. You definitely won't regret it—especially when you feel what it's like to truly *live*!

When you're setting up your Live part of the budget, list all the expenses you have each month: your mortgage/rent, utilities, groceries, gas, and so on. You also need to include all your debts, but your priority should be that you can eat, put a roof over your head, keep the lights on, and get to work.

The Luxury

This being said, here's where I've seen a lot of people get into trouble. I've helped many people set up a budget, and their cable/internet/cell phone bills were some of the most expensive items on their budget. I've never understood why someone has unlimited internet on their phone and unlimited Wi-Fi at home. This is a waste of money, especially when you're trying to keep from drowning. Therefore, these luxury items are one of the most important things to cut in your budget. This isn't a permanent decision; it's a temporary one. If you can do without now, you'll be able to get it back faster. Let me give you an example.

A few years ago I cut the cord on my cable. My wife wasn't watching TV, and my kids (who were ten and twelve at the time) watched only Netflix and Disney Plus. When I started looking at what I watched, most of it was the local channels. I made the decision to use my antenna for TV access. Then, on Black Friday, I bought a DVR and an Amazon Firestick for each TV. I then used the internet to stream the shows my family liked to watch.

This has worked for me for the last two years. I really haven't missed anything. The total monthly cost for my internet and TV has been $75 (that includes Netflix and Disney Plus). Rates for cable may vary, but I promise you'll save money if you cut the cord as I've done. Thus, the moral of the story is this: don't let your cable bill keep you from treading water. Don't let your cell phone bill keep you from moving forward. You can always go back and increase these when you get into better financial shape.

The Minimums

For your debts, find out what the minimum payments are for each one. That's all you need to pay at this time. The main focus should be to get that $1,000 emergency fund set up. We can worry about paying off that debt later. Keep your eye on the emergencies.

The hard part is that you're going to have to say no to some things for now. Maybe you can't go on vacation for a while. Maybe you can't spend a lot at Christmas. If you succumb to the temptation to spend your emergency fund, you might find yourself going backward. Saying no now will allow you to say yes later.

For example, I had to learn to say no to trading trucks. I had to learn to say no to going to the ATM multiple times a week. I had to learn to say no to having the newest cell phone. Saying no to all of these and more was one of the best decisions I've ever made.

At some point you'll tire of treading—but at least you aren't drowning! That's what you have to keep in mind. You'll find yourself repeating things like "I can't do this forever," and that's okay. I promise that this won't last much longer. Trust me: that feeling of being tired and discouraged all the time will dissipate.

Here's the best advice I can give you to keep you moving forward: do not quit or give up. That's just going to lead you back to drowning. As far as your family is concerned, when they see the progress you're making, they'll want to be a part of it too. So try to keep a positive attitude about it. If they don't join us, that's okay. You can't make them change their ways. Remember: you can change only yourself. When they see how happy and *unstressed* you are, they'll likely join in.

The Example of Jack and Diane

When we last met with Jack and Diane, they were drowning. They weren't giving, had very little in savings, and had no clue about the total of their monthly expenses. They had four debts: a truck payment, a student loan, a credit card, and a medical bill. I asked them to write down all their monthly expenses, and I noticed a couple of problems that mean once we correct everything, they'll be spending more than they bring home each month. So let's help get their heads above water and dive into the budget.

Again, below is the list of monthly expenses they wrote down for me. You'll notice that some of them are estimates, so it's going to take some time to get an exact amount. Here's the answer to a question you may have had for some time now: I always tell couples that they need three months to get a better idea on things likes groceries and gas. One or two months don't give you a good idea. The third month allows you to take the average.

1. Mortgage: $1,050
2. Utilities
   - Electric: $150 (average)
   - Water/Sewer: $100 (average)
   - Internet/Cable: $200
   - Cell Phones: $200
3. Truck Payment: $500
4. Student Loan: $125
5. Credit Card: $60
6. Medical Bill: $50

7. Car Insurance: $125
8. Groceries: $1,000 (estimate)
9. Gas: $200 (estimate)
10. Eating Out: $200 (estimate)

Total: $3,960

As you can see, two of their utilities are an average. I've often advised people to check with their utility companies to see if they can be on a budget billing service. I do this with my electric bill and gas bill. I pay the same amount for eleven months and then catch up on the twelfth bill. This keeps me from being surprised every month when I get the bill. Thus, to make this example easier, we're using $150 for electric and $100 for water/sewer. At some point, we'll need to add a few "other" expenses and make some cuts to certain areas of spending. At any rate, we also want to actually see where their money is going. So we're going to create their budget on a spreadsheet using the Give, Save, and Live method. Remember: our goal is to get from drowning to treading, so here we go!

How to Get Your Head Above Water

1. Give – give consistently each month
2. Save – save $1,000 for emergencies
3. Live – start living on a budget; pay the minimum payments on all debts

---

I usually do this on an Excel spreadsheet, but like I said earlier, you can do this however you like. The main thing to remember is to find something that's simple and works for you.

	Budget Expense	Amount
Give		
Save		
Live	Mortgage	$1,050
	Water/Sewer	$100
	Internet/Cable	$200
	Electric Bill	$150
	Car Insurance	$125
	Cell Phone	$200
	Truck Payment	$500
	Student Loan	$125
	Credit Card	$60
	Medical Bill	$50
	Groceries	$1,000
	Gas	$200
	Eating Out	$200
	Total	$3,960

Without putting anything down for Give and Save (for now), here's what I noticed as we talked further.

1. They've spent $3,960 out of $4,200 so far.
2. I found out that they have a dog but nothing is budgeted for pet supplies/pet care. Animals are expensive these days, so we'll have to budget something for vet bills, food, and so on. We'll use cash for this.
3. They also have nothing budgeted for vehicle maintenance (tires, oil changes, and so on). We'll use cash for this too.
4. They have two kids, and there are unavoidable expenses here. To keep kid-related expenses from getting out of control, this will be another cash expense.
5. Jack and Diane will have some unexpected things come up each month, so they need something for that. We won't be able to give them much, but this is needed. This is usually a cash expense to control expenses.
6. They were spending $200 a month eating out. We're going to reduce this amount and use cash here too.
7. We're going to have to make some cuts to make this work. The areas we're going to have to cut are cell phones and internet/cable.

Before moving on with the budget, I want to elaborate on numbers 2–6. Using cash for certain items was one of the best things I ever did when I started budgeting. I use cash for two reasons. First, cash is used for items that could get out of hand—spending, eating out, and so on. Second, cash is good to use for items I use several times a year but not necessarily every month. Some examples are vehicle maintenance and pet supplies. If I don't use the cash one month, I can keep building that up for when I get that big repair bill, vet bill, and so on. We still use cash today for a few budget items, like eating out. In fact, we'll probably always use cash for that. If we want to eat out and there's cash in the envelope, we eat out. If there's no cash in the envelope, we eat at home.

A word of advice here: I mentioned before that a couple of years ago I made some changes to save on cell phones, internet, and cable bills. Those expenses always frustrated me because I felt like they were too high and kept going up each month. We began using streaming services like Netflix for TV, and for our cell phones, we moved to a much cheaper pre-paid plan with limited data because, as I said, I've never understood having unlimited data on a cell phone when you have unlimited internet at home and possibly at work.

Now back to Jack and Diane. We need to make some changes to get their heads above water. Let's look at their updated budget. I've highlighted the budget items and amounts that were added or changed.

	Budget Expense	Amount
Give	**Church/Nonprofit/Etc.**	**$100**
Save	**Emergency Fund**	**$160**
Live	Mortgage	$1,050
	Water/Sewer	$100
	Internet/Cable	**$50**
	Electric Bill	$150
	Car Insurance	$125
	Cell Phone	**$125**
	Truck Payment	$500
	Student Loan	$125
	Credit Card	$60
	Medical Bill	$50
	Pet	**$25**
	Vehicle Maintenance	**$40**
	Kids' Needs	**$80**
	Jack's Spending	**$80**
	Diane's Spending	**$80**
	Eating Out	**$100**
	Groceries	$1,000
	Gas	$200
	Total	$4,200

As you can see, we've made the following changes:

1. They've decided to give $100 per month consistently.
2. They're saving $160 per month to put into their emergency fund. At this rate, it'll take them about six months to save the $1,000 they need to start treading. If they work extra jobs, this will happen more quickly.
3. They've made cuts to their internet/cable bill and their cell phone bill.
4. They've added six items they'll use cash for each month: pet, vehicle maintenance, kids' needs, Jack's spending, Diane's spending, and eating out.

Payday

Here's what Jack and Diane will do each month on payday. First, they'll pay all their one-time expenses. These are budget items you pay once a month and don't have to think about again until the next month. These include their giving, their saving, and their living from their mortgage down to their medical bill.

You might ask, "What if the bill isn't due until the middle or end of the month?" Great question. Go ahead and deduct this amount from your checking. That way, in your mind it's already paid. Then when you pay it online or it's due, you've already subtracted that amount and you don't have to worry about not having enough money.

After Jack and Diane take care of all their one-time expenses, then they get their cash for their envelopes (budget items "Pet" through "Eating Out"). They'll use this cash as needed during the month. You may wonder how to make that cash last all month. What I usually do is put half of it away until the middle of the month and then put it into my envelope. You have to be disciplined in this area. Don't spend your whole month's money in the first couple of weeks. Here's a tip: after you take out your cash, leave the money for gas and groceries in your checking account. As you go to the store or gas station, use your debit card to pay for those expenses.

So there you have it! Jack and Diane are heading toward treading. They're giving consistently and working toward that $1,000 emergency fund, they have a budget, and they're paying the minimum payments on all their debt. Once they get the $1,000 saved, they'll be treading water!

Challenge: One Step You Can Take Today

Set up your budget. Be sure to include some giving and saving. You want to give something consistently every month and need to save that $1,000 for emergencies. If your giving is lower than you want it to be, that's okay. The goal is to build it over time. Don't feel guilty. Before you know it, you'll be giving more than you ever thought possible if you stick with the plan. In your Live section, write down all your monthly expenses. You'll probably have to make some cuts. Making cuts isn't easy, but remember: they're temporary. Be sure to pay the minimum payment on all your debts. Remember: creating a budget is one of the hardest steps, but you can do this!

6

Swimming

"Walk with the wise and become wise; associate with fools and get in trouble."[7]

Now that you're treading and have some stability, it's time to get to the next step. I can remember treading water—at first it was fine because I knew I wasn't drowning, but I wanted to do more. Eventually I'd get tired and realize I couldn't do this forever. Learning to swim is a special time most everyone experiences. Most learn at a young age, but others don't learn how to swim until they're a lot older. I've met a few people who've never learned how to swim. The earlier you can learn, the better.

I can remember the freedom I experienced when I learned how to swim. I didn't have to wear the ring or arm floaties anymore. I could jump into the deep end from the side of the pool or off the diving board. I could come down the slide without the fear of drowning because I knew I could swim. I also remember that when my dad first threw me into the pool, I didn't become a strong swimmer immediately. Sure, I could stay above water for a few minutes, but I couldn't swim to the side of the pool very well. It took time to learn how to swim well. Once I learned, there was no fear.

It's the same way with our finances. You won't go from drowning to swimming overnight, especially if you have a lot of debt. It's going to take a while. But I promise that if you don't give up and you keep working on it, you'll be swimming before you know it. Then you'll start having the freedom you've always wanted with your finances—no more wearing a ring or those floaties on your arms. You'll be swimming like a champ.

Before you begin swimming—when you're treading with your finances—you're kind of stuck. You're not drowning, but you're also not moving forward. If you're treading, you now have a plan and you're not going deeper into debt each month. The bad thing is that you're not moving forward and you're not swimming—not yet! That's what this chapter will help you do: gain some mobility and swim! You do have to be careful because sometimes this can be a long step in the plan (depending on how much debt you have). I've seen people start swimming and then get discouraged or make a big mistake and go backward. Let's not let that happen.

Now it's time to step up your giving to 10 percent. The question a lot of people ask is "Do I give 10 percent of my gross pay or my take-home pay?" I believe the goal is to give 10 percent of your gross pay. You may have to start with 10 percent of your take-home pay, but you can gradually increase the amount as you're able.

Here's the way this works: if you make $48,000 per year, your gross amount is $4,000 per month. So you would give $400. You can choose to give the whole amount to one place or divide it up and give it to several places. The main point is to use your money to help make a difference in the lives of others.

> **GIVE:**
> **To move from treading to swimming, you have to start giving 10 percent of your income each month.**

I remember when I first started giving. It wasn't easy at first, but I quickly noticed that I was able to help make a difference in someone's life by giving. As I've mentioned, I would give of my time, and that's very important, but I started seeing that there were some cases when giving my money was the best way I could help certain people, nonprofits, my church, and so on. At any rate, it was a huge sacrifice for me to start giving 10 percent of my income. When I bumped my giving up to 10 percent, I started with take-home pay. That was a much easier transition for me.

One point to remember in giving is not to make it all about you. It's easy to want credit for giving. We like it when people acknowledge us for what we've done. I believe we should give and not get any credit for it at all. For example, I can remember Jamie and me going out to eat several years ago. The server was incredible, and I felt like I was supposed to give her a big tip. I left the tip, but I chose to walk slowly

SAVE:
To move from treading to swimming, you have to save one month of expenses in an emergency fund.

out the door so she could see me and know that I gave it to her. This isn't what giving is all about. I should've kept walking out the door, and that's all. It was funny, though, that the server came out the door crying. She told us that our tip was really going to help her because she was going through a really hard time. She hugged Jamie. My next thought was "I'm the one who left the tip. Why don't I get a hug?" I was being very selfish. It wasn't about me. It was about helping someone else. The point is this: when we give, it's important to give and not get credit for it. To me that's what giving is all about.

When you started treading, you had $1,000 saved in an emergency fund for emergencies. Wasn't that nice to have? Now it's time to grow that amount to one month of expenses. In our world, you need to be prepared not only for an emergency but also for losing your job.

When I was growing up it was common to see people stay at a job for thirty years. Now it seems like more and more people are being let go. There just doesn't seem to be as much loyalty these days. I've seen several of my friends work at a company for over twenty years and then one day be told they no longer have a job.

Why does this happen? Maybe it's because the company can hire someone else for much less pay. I'm not sure. What I am sure about, however, is that you must be prepared.

How Much Do You Need?

To figure out how much you need, take out your budget and see what amount you could live on for one month if you lost your job. Keep budget items like mortgage, utilities, gas, and groceries. You can remove items like eating out, cable, and so on. Picking which items to cut can be a tough decision. Now that you're trying to swim, you may have been able to add a few things back into your budget that you had to cut when you were drowning or treading, but just remember: things can change. I'm not saying that you have to totally cut these things from your budget; just be prepared if something crazy happens.

The fact of the matter is that emergencies can and will still happen. Sometimes they can get very expensive. I can remember building my savings up to $10,000 and I was so excited about it. Then the next thing I knew, I had a couple of things happen in my life and I made some stupid decisions. I turned around and what do you know? I had less than $1,000 in my savings. I took a step backward.

LIVE:

To move from treading to swimming, you have to be consistently living on a budget and be paying off your debts from smallest to largest.

Swimming can be a very rewarding place to be in this journey, but it can also be a very challenging place to be.

This can be one of the longest parts of the process if you have a lot of debt. It can also be a place to get distracted and move backward. I've seen couples who are swimming one month and then two months later they're treading water.

Here's what you have to know: when you go from treading to swimming, you have to watch out for two things. First, you have to make sure you're swimming in the right direction. You want to swim to safety, but that won't happen if you're swimming back toward danger. If you don't have a good budget to follow consistently, you could end up hurting yourself instead of helping.

Second, you have to watch out for obstacles that could get in your way. You have to keep your head up. It's easy to fall back into old ways. Here's a good example. I mentioned earlier in the book that I recently considered buying another truck. This was really tempting for me because my current truck is twelve years old. I'm thankful I didn't make a quick decision. I was able to realize that I really didn't need a newer truck.

Also, sometimes I'll start looking at houses online. It can get very tempting to move to a new house. I love where I live, but I would like to have a one-level house. There are also a few other things I'd like to change about my house. I get online and start seeing other houses for sale. My family moved a lot when I was a kid. It became normal to us to move to another house. Thankfully, houses are way too expensive right now, which keeps me from moving. The last thing I need is to increase my mortgage and house payment. I could get a bigger house, but that's not what we need as a family right now.

Here's the major point: don't let the desire to buy a new house or vehicle keep you from swimming in the right direction. You'll probably regret it later. Stick with your plan!

There was one couple I met with a few times. They started out barely treading, but we were headed in the right direction. They had no debt except the house and had gotten some money from a family member that dramatically increased their savings. We had a plan and things were going well. Then I didn't hear from them for a few months.

When we met again, things had changed a lot. They barely had their heads above water. They had two car payments and no money in savings. The guy's company wasn't going to provide a vehicle anymore, so he financed a brand-new car. The wife got jealous and wanted a brand-new car too. Now they had two car payments each month, $500 each. That was very discouraging because now they were in worse shape than when they began.

On the other hand, I've seen several couples use their time of swimming and totally change their lives. Many times I've gotten a text from a couple telling me they've paid off another debt. That's so exciting. That's a big goal during swimming: pay off your debts one at a time.

One couple came to me a couple of years ago. They made good money but had a lot of debt. On the other hand, they didn't have a plan and felt like they were heading in the wrong direction. They weren't giving anything, but they did have some savings in the bank. So I helped them set up a budget and we got a plan to start giving and paying down their debt. It was so much fun to watch them work together and get themselves into a better spot financially. Every time we met, they'd paid off another debt. I learned that it can really bond a couple together when they're focused on the same goal. I remember when they paid off their last debt and all they had left was their house payment. They were so excited and were in a great position to start using their money for bigger and better things instead of paying off debt each month.

Paying Off the Debt

You might ask these questions: How do I pay these debts off? Which one do I pay off first? Some will say to pay off the one with the highest interest rate first. I totally disagree and here's why. Paying off debts is exciting. That's what's going to motivate you to keep going. If you start off with five debts, you want to get to four, then three, and so on. The easiest debt to pay off is the one with the smallest amount.

Here's what you do: list your debts from smallest to largest based on what you owe. On your budget, pay the minimum payment on all of these except for the smallest one. With this one, pay as much extra as you can. So if your minimum payment is $25 and you have an extra $50 to put toward that payment, now pay $75 a month. This will allow you to pay it off faster. When this debt is paid off, take that $75 and add that amount to the next smallest debt and pay that off.

I've seen people over the years start adding an extra $50 a month to the smallest debt. By the time they get to debt number four or five, they are paying an extra $500 to that amount. Imagine how fast a debt goes away by adding an extra $500 each month.

I love hearing from couples when they pay off a debt. I can tell that they're getting more excited each time they pay one off. It's like adding fuel to the fire for them. It keeps them moving in the right direction. It can be the same way for you!

One thing you can do if you want to pay off your debts faster is working an extra side job or two. I'll never forget all the extra jobs I worked to help pay off debt faster. I worked as a math tutor, I delivered newspapers early in the morning, and I mowed yards on Saturdays. I know there were a few more. The good news is that I don't have to do that anymore. Working all those extra jobs motivated me not to get into debt anymore.

Your Reality Now: Being Honest

Hopefully by now you're learning to consistently live on a budget and living on less than you make. I also hope you're learning to communicate with your spouse if you're married. Communication is key in any relationship, especially marriage. If you want to be successful in the financial journey, you have to be honest with your spouse.

A few years ago I was helping a couple with their finances. Everything seemed to be going well, but there was something that didn't feel right. The husband was all in and wanted to get everything paid off. The wife was very quiet and didn't seem all in. They stopped coming to see me after a few meetings, and later I found out why. They weren't communicating at all, and the wife wasn't being honest about her finances. Tragically that marriage ended in divorce a few months later.

That one broke my heart. I never want to see a couple get divorced. That situation just reminded me about the importance of good communication. Like I said earlier, when you're swimming you have to watch out for obstacles that get in your way. That is definitely one of those obstacles.

The Example of Jack and Diane

Let's get back to our example of Jack and Diane. So far we've helped them get from drowning to treading by making their giving consistent, saving $1,000 in their emergency fund, setting up a budget that's more than just numbers on a page, and making sure they're paying their minimum payments on their debts. Their heads are above water and they can breathe.

As we know with treading water, it's not something we can do forever. You eventually get tired and could possibly drown. We have to get Jack and Diane moving forward by swimming. They've turned around and started heading toward the shallow water, and we need to make sure they keep swimming the right way and help them watch out for obstacles that could cause them to take a step backward. When you're new to budgeting, it's easy to fall back into old habits. Let's not let that happen to Jack and Diane or to you. So what do we need to do?

1. We need them to get their giving up to 10 percent.
2. We need them to save one month of expenses in their emergency fund.
3. We need them to be living consistently on this budget and start paying down their debt.

You may ask, "What order do I need to do these three things in?" I don't have an answer that works for everyone. The most obvious answer is to pay down the debt first and then add to your giving and savings. If you start working extra jobs, you could put all that extra money on the debt or put some in each of the three categories. For this example, we'll pay the debt off first. That gives us confidence to keep moving forward.

Which debt do we attack first? The smallest one. That'll be the easiest one to tackle. Since Jack and Diane have their $1,000 saved for emergencies, we're going to take a break on saving and add that money to our debt payment. We aren't going to stop giving, though.

The smallest debt is their medical bill ($2,000 balance). They've been paying $50 a month for their minimum payment. We're going to stop the saving and add that $160 a month to the $50 for a new payment of $210 a month.

Also, Jack has decided to work an extra job delivering pizzas at night. By working a few extra hours a week, Jack is bringing home an extra $300 a month. This brings their monthly total to $4,500. He's going to put that money toward his medical bill. (Changes bolded on next page.) Now they'll pay $510 a month toward the medical bill.

I also want to point out that Jack and Diane will probably get raises at their jobs over time. If that happens, they'll add the extra money on their check to the smallest debt. However, to keep this example simpler, we won't add in any raises. So let's take a look at what we've got:

	Budget Expense	**Amount**
Give	Church/Nonprofit/Etc.	$100
Save	**Emergency Fund**	**$0**
Live	Mortgage	$1,050
	Water/Sewer	$100
	Internet/Cable	$50
	Electric Bill	$150
	Car Insurance	$125
	Cell Phone	$125
	Truck Payment	$500
	Student Loan	$125
	Credit Card	$60
	Medical Bill ($2K balance)	**$510**
	Pet	$25
	Vehicle Maintenance	$40
	Kids' Needs	$80
	Jack's Spending	$80
	Diane's Spending	$80
	Eating Out	$100
	Groceries	$1,000
	Gas	$200
	Total	$4,500

With these changes, the medical bill will be paid off in four months. That's when this starts getting exciting. Instead of five debts, now they have four!

What's Next?

Now that the medical bill is gone, we're going to attack the next debt. Yes: the credit card with a minimum payment of $60 and a total of $5,000. We'll add the $510 from the medical bill to the $60 payment and start paying $570 a month. Everything else stays the same. See only the updated debts below:

Truck Payment	$500
Student Loan	$125
Credit Card	**$570**

The credit card should now take eight or nine months to pay off. Then they'll be down to three debts! The next step is to take that $570 and add to the $125 student loan debt for a new total of $695. See below:

Truck Payment	$500
Student Loan	**$695**

The student loan should be paid off in seventeen months. Finally, add the $695 from the student loan to the $500 truck payment for a new total of $1,195. Now they can pay off the truck in sixteen to seventeen months.

Truck Payment $1,195

Once they get the truck paid off, then it'll be time to increase their giving to 10 percent and savings to one month of expenses. Jack and Diane will take the $1,195 from the truck payment and add that to their giving and saving. That's how they'll get from swimming to wading—which is the best part of your journey!

I know this seems like it's taken a long time, but it goes by more quickly than you think. If you can put extra money toward it as you're able, it'll disappear even faster. The important thing is that you're making progress.

Challenge: One Step You Can Take Today

Now that you're consistently giving each month, you have $1,000 in your emergency fund, and you're paying the minimum payments on all your debts, it's time to start paying down that debt. List all your debts from smallest to largest. Pay the minimum payment on all of them except the smallest one. Use the money you were saving each month and add that to the payment of the smallest debt payment. For example, if your smallest debt monthly payment is $25/month and you were saving $50/month, now your payment will be $75/month. When you pay this debt off, add that $75/month to the next debt and pay that one off more quickly. Repeat this cycle until the only debt you have left is your house payment.

7

Wading

"The generous will prosper; those who refresh others will themselves be refreshed."[8]

Now that you're swimming, the next goal is to get into the shallow water where you can wade around and relax. This is where the fun begins. My town of Hendersonville, Tennessee, has Old Hickory Lake running beside it. Years ago I was on a boat with some others and in the distance I saw a bunch of boats together and a volleyball net. All these teenagers were wading in the shallow water playing volleyball. Nowhere else in this lake could that be done. I later found out that area is called "Two Foot" because it's so shallow. What a great place to wade around. They were having a blast. That's the kind of fun we all deserve.

I can remember being in the ocean and turning around to swim toward the beach. I couldn't wait to get there. I knew once I got into the shallow water, my life was going to change. That's where I could stand up and relax. That's where people were having fun. They were throwing Frisbees, body surfing, and running around. When it comes to our finances, that's what we're aiming for: to be in the shallow water where we can have a great time free from worries.

I thought I'd share this with you, however: I used to think this stage of the financial game was "running" instead of "wading." I thought the final goal was to get out of the water so you could "run" and feel free. A couple of friends of mine shared some great wisdom with me and I'm so glad I listened. They said, "Jason, you'll never get out of the water. You'll always have some kind of financial issue. The issues are just different when the water is at your knees instead of over your head."

This blew my mind and they were so right. Even though you're now going in a good financial direction, things come up on a regular basis. Just because you've been able to give and save more doesn't mean surprises won't happen. When these surprises do happen, it'll still hurt, but you'll be more prepared because you aren't headed back to the dangerous water where you could drown. With that being said, dangers lurk everywhere—even in the shallows.

Still, Be Careful Though

When you're in the shallow water, there are a few things you have to watch out for. First, you still have to watch out for the waves. They can still knock you down if you're not careful. Second, you could still get sucked back into the deeper water if you're not careful. You have to pay attention to how strong the undertow is that day. One day it's not bad and the next it is. You always have to be aware of your surroundings.

Next you have to be on the lookout for certain animals swimming around you (like jellyfish, sharks, or stingrays). I can remember a time in college when I swam out in the deeper water at night not thinking a thing about it. Now as a forty-six-year-old man, I'm always wondering what's swimming around my legs. I guess that comes with age.

Finally you have to make sure you're still in line with your family and their tent, chairs, and other beach gear. It's easy to drift away and then realize you're several yards away from your family. Keep an eye on your loved ones and your surroundings! Don't get swept away, my friends.

Compared to drowning, however, these issues are completely different when you're wading. The goal is not to become overconfident. You've made a lot of progress and you should be proud of yourself, but still, you have to be careful. You have to know your goals and always make sure you're in alignment. If you get out of line, you need to make corrections quickly instead of waiting and ending up back over your head in deep water.

When you get to this point financially, you'll realize that the work was well worth it. You can live a whole different life when you're in the shallow water. Now that you've made that 180-degree turn financially, you're a different person and you never want to go back to the way things used to be. Things that were once important to you aren't as important anymore. You don't care about keeping up with the Joneses because they're in debt. You're free to do things you've always wanted to do. Trust me, in my life I've been drowning, treading, swimming, and wading. Wading is by far the best place to be. I never want to go backward.

The biggest thing I've learned is that I'm always going to have financial questions and issues in my life. Things are going to happen that I didn't expect. I'm going to make mistakes. My kids are fourteen and twelve and I have no clue what'll happen in the future. What I do know is that I can handle it much better when I'm knee deep in the water instead of having the water over my head. I hope what I've been showing you will motivate you to keep your eye on the prize. I promise you won't regret all the sacrifices and hard work. With that being said, let's take a look at what it takes to get to the shallow waters of "Two Foot."

GIVE:

To move from swimming to wading, you have to start giving above and beyond what you ever thought possible.

Now it's time to really step up your giving. Hopefully you've been giving 10 percent of your gross income for a while and your life has been completely changed. Your budget looks so different than it did when you first started—you actually have one and are sticking to it. You can choose to do a lot of things with your money, but one of those things should be to start giving *more* than 10 percent. One realistic goal could be to increase it a little each year—maybe by one or two percent. Also, when you get a raise it's definitely a good idea to give more then.

You may ask this question: Jason, why do you focus so much on giving? Let me put it this way: I've spoken at several funerals during my life. I've never seen a funeral procession with a U-Haul behind the hearse. The point is that you can't take it with you. We should want to do things that'll make an impact in people's lives long after we're gone. This is how we do it: by giving.

I've worked at churches and nonprofits for most of my professional career. There are some organizations and people who are really making a difference in our world. Now that you've been blessed and can give more, let's do it. A lot of nonprofits struggle each year to make budget. They're doing a great work and need people like you and me to give of our time and money. Now you can partner with them and be a part of their mission.

To Give Is a Blessing for All

In the last twenty years, I've learned so much about giving. One of the ways I've learned is by watching how others handle the money they've been blessed with. I have a friend named Ryan who lives in East Tennessee. He's a giver in so many ways and he gives above and beyond. Ryan's always giving of his time. He's always willing to help someone no matter how much time it's going to take. Ryan and his wife are always ministering to people in their community. They host Bible studies at their house and are always willing to step in and counsel someone who's struggling. Ryan also gives of his money. He supports his church and other ministries including the nonprofit I work for. The cool thing is that he never complains about doing it and many times he does it anonymously.

As for me personally, working for nonprofit ministries all these years has allowed me to meet people who give over and beyond. There are some good people out there that have either made a lot of money, been smart with the money they have, or both. I could name so many people who have shown me examples of how to give, but they'd get mad because I said their name. Again, they don't give to receive recognition. They give because that's what they're supposed to do: they do so cheerfully, and they do so because it's a blessing for all.

I'm really trying to give over and beyond. While I was in my twenties and thirties, I'd go to breakfast or lunch with an older friend and they'd pick up the tab. Even in my forties, guys will pick up the tab. I'm starting to do this more and more—not to impress them or make myself look good but because I want to give back. I want to help others like so many did for me. Here's the thing: if I were drowning or even treading, there's no way I could do this. One advantage to wading is that you can budget money to help others. Jamie and I both have money budgeted each month that we use to help others or do something nice for them. We don't want anything in return. It's the best part of my budget.

Congratulations! You should be getting to a really good place with your savings. When you started swimming, you had one month of expenses saved in your emergency fund. Now it's time to grow it from one month to three to six months of expenses. Same principle: you never know when you might need it. Emergencies happen in life. That's just the way it is. Let me give you a good example.

I was so thankful for our emergency fund back in 2019. After working for a company for thirteen years, I found myself in the middle of an unexpected career change. I was still hoping to do my current job part-time but that didn't work out. My new job was great but I took a 40-percent pay cut. That's substantial! If it hadn't been for our strong budgeting and emergency fund, we would've been in trouble. Sure, we had to cut out some of our budget items, but we were fine.

Now, the good news was that over the next year and a half my salary grew to what it had been before. We tried to be smart with this money. Most of it went to giving and savings. We stuck to our budget and got back in the shallow end, where we could bask in the waters of old "Two Foot." So it all worked out.

SAVE:

To move from swimming to wading, you have to save three to six months of expenses in an emergency fund.

Do I Need a Piggy Bank?

There's a question you may be asking at this point: after I save my three- to six-month emergency fund, what do I do with all that money? Do I keep it in the bank? Do I have cash in a piggy bank? Where do I keep it all? Great question.

The idea here is that because it's for emergencies, you'll want to keep part of it at your bank so that you can get easy access to it. You'd want to get an account with the highest interest rate possible. The problem these days is that you won't be getting much interest at the bank. That's okay, though. The rest of your emergency fund can be put into a brokerage account. You'll need to see a financial advisor to set this up.

Why put it in a brokerage account? A brokerage account has allowed us to get more bang for our buck. We get a higher interest rate than we do at the bank. Plus, there's no penalty for taking the money out. It just may take a few days to get it. Finally, and most importantly, it separates our money so that it's not all in one place.

Now What?

Now, you might be asking, what do I do once I've saved my six months of expenses? Another great question. Once you've saved your emergency fund, it's time to get serious about your retirement. For example, after we got our six-month emergency fund together, we started putting money into an IRA. You have two choices with an IRA. There's a traditional IRA and a Roth IRA. My choice has always been the Roth IRA because your taxes are already paid when you put money into this account. With a traditional IRA, your balance will definitely look bigger, but you'll still have to pay taxes when you take the money out one day.

Other Savings

What else can you be saving for? What's next? We're saving for things like vacation, Christmas, holidays, and birthdays. We actually have different accounts at the bank where we save for these things. Online banking makes this so easy. When we get paid, we move money into our vacation account each month. This way we know that the money in that account is just for vacation. We do the same for Christmas and holidays.

It's so nice to be saving for all these things. Come January you can start saving for the next Christmas instead of paying off the previous Christmas. This really gives you peace of mind.

We're also saving each month for a car. My daughter is currently fourteen, so she'll be driving in two years. As I mentioned earlier in the book, the plan is to give her my wife's car. Now we can start saving for a new(er) car for Jamie. In that amount of time, we should be able to save enough to find her a really good used car—not a new one but newer than what she has now. Again, we use a different account for this. It's up to you what you save for, but just remember to use a different account for it. It makes life easy.

> **LIVE:**
> **To move from swimming to wading, you have to pay off your debt (minus the house) and be investing in the future instead of paying off the past.**

I'm so excited that you're getting out of the deep water into the shallow water. Imagine being in the ocean and being able to touch the bottom. As you walk toward the shore, the water gets lower and lower on your body. Eventually the water is at your waist, then at your knees. This is a game-changer. You feel a sense of freedom. You've been in the deep water for so long and the waves have worn you out. You don't have to worry about that anymore. You look back at the deep water and know that you don't ever want to get back in there again.

Although there's much relief here in the shallows, you still have to be careful. You have to watch out for the waves and not let yourself get sucked back into the deep water. You have to approach your finances the same way. Debt can suck you in and beat you down. Remember how you went from drowning to barely having your head above water? You don't want to go through that again. Be vigilant. Watch out for dangers.

Just be wise in the decisions you make. As we've discussed, your giving and saving amounts have increased a lot. On the other hand, you should see that your living amount has decreased. Your only debt is the house. All that money you were spending on debt can now be used to give and save. You also may be able to do some things you've always wanted to do, but just remember: keep moving forward. Keep wading.

The Old 10-10-80

Remember the 10-10-80 plan, where you give 10 percent and save 10 percent of your income and live off

80 percent of it? Where are you now compared to when you started? I can remember when we first started that our living amount was much more than 80 percent. I love to look at it now; we're so blessed to be living on so much less. I never want to go back to the way things used to be. I like to say that now we're investing in the future instead of paying off the past.

The Housing Question

Some have asked me if they should now pay off their house. I remember asking some buddies of mine this question a few years ago. All these guys had been wading for a long time. Half of them told me to pay it off and half told me not to. I've learned that it all depends on your situation. For us, we've chosen not to pay it off at this time.

Here's why: right now we have a $650 house payment and owe only around $65,000 on our house. If we pay it off, we'll still have to pay taxes and insurance each month, which amounts to roughly half of our payment. We've instead chosen to max out our retirement, and we're saving for a car when my daughter turns sixteen. Before I know it, we'll be working on a plan for what my son will drive. The next step is to save more for college; then we'll likely attack the house.

At this point we haven't saved a lot for college but it's our desire to do more of that. I know that college will be here quickly, but we've chosen to put money into our retirement. The reason for that is that kids have so many more options today when going to college. In Tennessee, students can go to community college for almost nothing these days. I don't want to pay for my kids' college and then struggle to make it when we retire. I think both can be done if you're smart with your money.

You've Come a Long Way, Champ

Think about where you are now. You're making statements like "Now I can . . . ." You can do things you never thought possible. You may also be saying, "I want others to experience this." Share your experiences with others. Encourage them! Tell them what it's like!

I believe we go through tough times in life for two reasons. The first one is that we grow as people during these times. When times are easy, we really don't grow. When times are tough, we have to makes changes and sacrifices. These growing pains are important because we find ourselves accomplishing goals we never thought possible. We push ourselves through these tough times and make ourselves into stronger people as long as we don't give up.

The second reason is that we can help others grow when they go through what we previously experienced. For example, when I'm going through a tough time, I look for someone in my life who can relate. I look for someone who's a few steps ahead of me. I don't want someone who's right where I am in the process. I want someone who's experienced the toughest part and who I can tell is a different person than they were before. I can tell that they're stronger. So, like I said, let others know the joy you've experienced on this journey. Help them by making a difference in their lives like someone once did for you.

The Example of Jack and Diane

We've been following Jack and Diane since they were drowning financially. First we got their heads above water so that they were treading. Then we got them to start swimming and getting their debt all paid off. Now it's time to get them wading in the shallow waters of "Two Foot."

Jack and Diane have finally finished paying off all their debts except the house. Jack has decided to quit delivering pizzas, so they're back to bringing home $4,200/month. On the following page is their updated budget:

They're currently giving and saving 10 percent of the net pay (take-home pay). With the money left over, we increased the following budget items: kids' spending, Jack's spending, Diane's spending, and eating out. Remember: it's okay to reward yourself a little as you accomplish big goals in your budget. Just make sure you don't forget about your goals.

See how much simpler this budget looks now? Jack and Diane are no longer paying hundreds of dollars toward debt. Plus, they can give more and save more instead of paying off debts each month. So now what do we need to do to get them wading? The first goal is to save the three to six months of expenses in an emergency fund. Jack and Diane have set a goal to save $12,000, which is very close to three months.

After they get this saved, they want to increase their giving to 10 percent of their gross income instead of their net income. Remember: your gross income is what you make before taxes. You net income is the amount of your check after everything has been taken out. Therefore, you'll be giving more when you give from your gross income. Jack and Diane make $60,000 a year (or $5,000 month). So they want to give $500 a month. As their situation continues to improve and they make more money, they can start giving above and beyond the 10 percent.

	Budget Expense	Amount
Give	Church/Nonprofit/Etc.	$420
Save	Emergency Fund	$420
Live	Mortgage	$1,050
	Water/Sewer	$100
	Internet/Cable	$50
	Electric Bill	$150
	Car Insurance	$125
	Cell Phone	$125
	Pet	$25
	Vehicle Maintenance	$40
	Kids' Needs	**$125**
	Jack's Spending	**$125**
	Diane's Spending	**$125**
	Eating Out	**$120**
	Groceries	$1,000
	Gas	$200
	Total	$4,200

Challenge: One Step You Can Take Today

After you get all your debt paid off, it's time to increase your giving and saving. The goals are to eventually give more than 10 percent of your income and ultimately save three to six months of expenses in your emergency fund. This may take a while, but remember: you aren't wasting any money paying debt each month. Feels good, doesn't it?

8

I'm Wading: What's Next?

"Joyful is the person who finds wisdom, the one who gains understanding. For wisdom is more profitable than silver, and her wages are better than gold. Wisdom is more precious than rubies; nothing you desire can compare with her."[9]

So now you're wading and you've come a long way. Congratulations! You may be wondering now: What's the next step? I know you're probably thinking there are so many more things that you want to do. How about a nice swim? Better yet, when I think about my favorite times in the water, they all involve wading. When I think about the times I was drowning, treading, or swimming, all I can think about is how scared or exhausted I was. I don't remember scary times when I was wading. Sure, I can remember falling because of the slippery rocks, but I was able to get back up and move on with my life.

I remember a time in college when I jumped off the high diving board. I'd never been on a high dive like this one. I was scared but I wasn't about to turn around and go back down the stairs. I jumped off the board and landed on my back. I was hurt and embarrassed. All I wanted to do was get back to the shallow end as quickly as possible. I was never going to do that again.

My times of drowning, treading, and swimming financially were stressful and difficult too. My best memories have come when I've been wading. This is where the fun is. This is where you can really make an impact with the money you've been given. Sure, I've made some stupid decisions with my finances. I stepped out on that high dive and knew I needed to go back, but I was so worried about what others might say. I jumped off and landed on my back only to regret what I'd just done. You live and you learn. The best lesson is to do what's best for you and your family. Don't worry about what others say or think. When you mess up, turn around, get back on track, and don't do that again. This being said, let's look at some possible next steps below using Give, Save, and Live.

Give:
Now that you can give more than 10 percent, what can you do?

Now that we have the freedom to do so, each month Jamie and I give to several different things. For example, we give money to our church, but we also support friends who have to raise support working for a nonprofit. As someone who's worked in the nonprofit world for years, I can say it's nice to be able to help others.

We also have "Other Giving" each month. Some of this money is left in our checking account and some of it is taken out as cash. Each month there are needs that arise that we don't know are coming. Having this extra money allows us to meet these unexpected needs. Someone in our lives may lose a loved one and we want to get them a meal. Another person may have had surgery and we want to provide them dinner. It's just nice to be able to help make a difference for those in our lives who are struggling.

Like I've said over and over, the Giving part of our budget is my favorite. There's no limit to the types of things you can give to. In case you're running out of ideas, here's a good list of things you might consider:

1. Giving to your church
2. Donating to a nonprofit/charity you're passionate about
3. Supporting your child's school/favorite teacher/athletic team
4. Giving a bigger tip to a server who does a great job
5. Paying for lunch for a friend who's always been there for you

6. Helping out a family in your community who are struggling by giving them money or paying their rent/utility bill

7. Taking a meal to a friend/family who just had surgery/has been sick

8. Paying for the meal of the person behind you in a drive-thru or a family at a restaurant

9. Buying grocery store gift cards and passing them out to random people at the store

Remember: you can still give of your time too. Just because you're in a different position financially doesn't mean you shouldn't give of your time anymore.

> **Save:**
> **Now that you have your three to six months of expenses saved for emergencies, you might be asking, "What do I save for now?"**

Years ago I noticed three things that were big hits to us financially each year and I wanted to be better prepared for them. Those things were vacation, Christmas, and birthdays. I knew when they were coming and they were coming every year. I honestly got to the point where I didn't like returning from vacation knowing I still had to pay it off when I got back. The same kind of thing happened after Christmas: I didn't like looking at that bill in January. It made me think about drowning. So I wanted to figure out a way to start paying for them earlier.

At first I thought I would put extra money into a savings account for all of these. That worked okay but it was hard to remember how much of the money was for Christmas and how much was for vacation. I thought about it, so here's what I did.

I went to the bank and opened up a couple of extra savings accounts. One of them I called Vacation and the other I called Christmas/Birthdays. This way I could move money into those accounts each month and know how much was in each one. Years later, I can say that this is one of the best decisions I've ever made. I save all year for Christmas, vacation, and birthdays. When I'm going to have an expense, I move that money back to checking or take it out in cash and pay for it.

Our bank accounts are like a wheel. Our checking account is the hub with spokes going to our other accounts: Emergency Fund, Vacation, Christmas/Holidays, and so on.

Here's a tip: make sure when you set up these accounts that they're free accounts. You don't want to be paying service fees each month.

The Retirement Thing

Another thing to be saving for is retirement. You may be contributing each month to your work's 401K but want to do something else. As I've mentioned, Jamie and I each have a Roth IRA and we've gradually increased that amount over the years. If you choose to do this, find a trusted financial advisor in your area and they'll help you set it up. Remember to talk to your advisor about the differences between a traditional IRA and a Roth IRA as we discussed in the last chapter.

Saving for the Kids

I started a savings account for my kids too. Most months they have expenses come up like art camp, basketball fees, and soccer fees. It doesn't happen every month, but I can let this money grow; then it's there when I need it.

Having a savings account for the kids has been very beneficial for us. As kids get older, so do their costs and involvement in activities. Many times these expenses are unpredictable too. For example, my daughter was just elected Homecoming Attendant for her freshman class. What an honor this was! We weren't planning on these expenses, but we're not going to tell her no. Thankfully we have the money saved in her account for a dress, shoes, hair appointment, and whatever else she might need for that.

LIVE:
The key thing to remember about your living is not to fall back into old habits.

This also allows us to teach our kids about saving money. If they want something, they need to save for it. I'm trying to teach them how to give, save, and live when they get money. The living part comes easily for them, but the giving and saving are tougher. When they ask us about buying something, I'll ask how much they have saved. Sometimes I may be willing to pay for part of it, but they need to be willing to pay for the other part out of their savings. Bottom line: I hope they're learning that they can't buy anything until they have the money saved to pay for it.

Hopefully you've learned by now that you don't need the things you once thought were essential. You've learned that paying too much for cable and cell phones each month isn't necessary. You'll learn this too: your cars will get old and you'll need another one. Your kids will get old enough to drive and you'll need to buy one for them. When this happens, remember how much you can waste on a new car. As I said at the beginning of this book, I used to trade trucks all the time. Now I own a twelve-year-old truck with over 200,000 miles. Jamie owns a ten-year-old SUV with over 100,000 miles. They work perfectly and we don't desire brand-new cars. The point is this: cars are an easy way to blow your budget. The idea is to get from point A to point B. It isn't a fashion show. Be humble and take a donkey if you have to. Really: drive what you can afford.

Love Your Life and Live Your Best

The lower your living expenses are, the more you can give and save. Now, I'm not saying you can't afford to do some things for yourself. That's totally fine. Just be wise in what you do. Live your best life and love it, but don't forget about the future.

As for the future, you want to make sure you have enough life insurance. You may have some at your job and that's great, but you need to have some personally too. If you leave your job or lose your job, that insurance won't transfer with you. If something happens to you or your spouse, you don't want your family to struggle. I always recommend term life insurance instead of whole life insurance. The first reason is because it's cheaper and will work better in your budget. The second reason is because when the term is up, you can reevaluate how much you need based on where you are with your budget. One of my long-term goals is to decrease the amount of life insurance I need. When my kids get out of college and our house is paid off, I won't need as much insurance as I have now.

Challenge: One Step You Can Take Today

A lot has happened in your life in last few months or even years. You may have been drowning when you first started this process. Now you're wading. What do you do now? It's time to pass all of this on to someone else. I know there's someone in your life who's drowning financially. It's time to pass this knowledge on to them. If there's one thing you can do today—or every day—help someone else change their lives for the better like you've changed yours.

I have one last story I want to share with you. There's a couple in Hendersonville whom I met two years ago. Let's call them Tim and Sherry. This couple was drowning. They had a lot of debt and weren't communicating at all. They didn't really trust each other when it came to their finances. Tim and Sherry were spending $500/month in marriage counseling and had filed for divorce. They had no plan in place. I met with them about fifteen times over a year. We got them on a plan and they started moving forward. I saw them recently at a high school football game. They're still married and are doing well. The last thing they told me at the game was "We have no debt now! We've paid it all off!" They were so excited to be where they are and they're still moving in the right direction. I'm so thankful I was able to help them. I hope this book has done the same for you.

Here's my goal: I want to use my time on earth to impact the lives of others. I want to help people. I want to be unselfish with my time and resources. I urge you to do the same. The more people are struggling in one area, the more it can impact the other parts of their lives. The same goes for helping them with their finances: a little bit of help can go a long way. With that being said, I hope this book will help you, but also help you help others. Life is too short, so just be willing to help someone. As you help them, remember to continue to love them and be there for them no matter what happens. Life is complicated, after all. That's why I will leave you with this: keep it simple, friends.

Notes

1. Proverbs 19:20
2. Proverbs 4:25–27
3. Brady, Tom. *60 Minutes*. By Steve Kroft. CBS, November 4, 2006.
4. Proverbs 13:10
5. Proverbs 15:22
6. Proverbs 25:28
7. Proverbs 13:20
8. Proverbs 11:25
9. Proverbs 3:13–15

Made in the USA
Middletown, DE
11 March 2022